THE
PURPOSE
OF THE
Dance

VOLUME 1

THE
PURPOSE
OF THE
Dance

VOLUME 1

DR. ANN HIGGINS

iUniverse, Inc.
New York Lincoln Shanghai

The Purpose Of The Dance
VOLUME 1

iUniverse books may be ordered through booksellers or by contacting:

iUniverse
2021 Pine Lake Road, Suite 100
Lincoln, NE 68512
www.iuniverse.com
1-800-Authors (1-800-288-4677)

Because of the dynamic nature of the Internet, any Web addresses or links contained in this book may have changed since publication and may no longer be valid.

Cover Design & Layout by:
Marlon & Joanne Nicolls
www.marlonicolls.com

ISBN: 978-0-595-48174-3 (pbk)
ISBN: 978-0-595-60271-1 (ebk)

Printed in the United States of America

CONTENTS

CHAPTER 1

GOD IS A GOD OF MOVEMENT

In the beginning God created the heavens and the earth. And the earth was without form and void; and darkness was upon the face of the deep, and the spirit of God moved upon the face of the waters. (Genesis 1:1-2)

God is a God of movement. The Spirit of God moved upon the face of the waters and transformed an earth that was without form and void, into a spectacular array of beauty filled with movement. In verse 20 of Genesis chapter 1, God said,

"… Let the waters bring forth abundantly the moving creature that hath life.…"

In verse 21 God created great whales and every living creature that moved …

God is a Triune God. He made man in His image and likeness, therefore, man is tripartite: Body, Soul & Spirit. When God formed man from the dust of the ground, He was putting man together out of something. The Greek word for form is asha which means to make out of something. We see some of the parts in man talked about in Genesis 2:22. God took a rib out of man; in verse 23 we see man had bones and flesh. When God put man together He made the body in a way that man can be flexible and moveable. He put joints in different sections of our body to cause us to be able to move in every direction possible. Man was able to walk, to bend, to stoop, kick, jump, twirl and turn because of flexibility. That's how God formed man from the beginning. God breathed life into man so that he can move. When we were commanded to praise God in the dance in Psalms 150:4 and 149:3, David had already experienced the joy of movement. David had experienced the spirit of death and the spirit of life. The Word says that a merry heart is good like a medicine but a broken spirit driest up the bones. In Psalm 51 David had his spirit renewed, so when he danced before the Lord, it was out of a new spirit. He was releasing the glory of God; he was rejoicing.

One of the Hebrew words for dance and rejoice is Karar, meaning to whirl, or to move in a circle like David did in 2 Samuel 6:4. David danced before the Lord in worship with all his might.

In Gen. 1:2 the Spirit of God moved upon the face of the earth and something wonderful happened. It brought light and life. When the Spirit of God moved upon David who was an earthen vessel, something wonderful happened. He was full of joy and he began to worship.

The lifting of our hands and bowing down before the Lord are demonstrations of a heart surrendered and expressions of the inner man being poured out through physical movements of the body. Every member of your body has an important role in praising and worshipping the Lord: the head, the hands, the feet, etc.

Every creature God placed on this earth has a creative movement. It's in God we live and move and have our being. I am blessed to be living in the Bahamas near the beautiful blue waters where I can watch some of God's wonderful creatures show forth His glory.

One night I went to dinner with a group of our dancers at a beautiful hotel on the waters, and after we ate, the dancers decided to take a tour around the hotel. We started walking around a large aquarium that had fishes of every size and color; it had lobsters and sea plants. The amazing part that almost blew us away as we watched was the fishes as they began to move in unison. They created patterns and diagrams as they gracefully moved and the choreographic nature of God became very obvious to us.

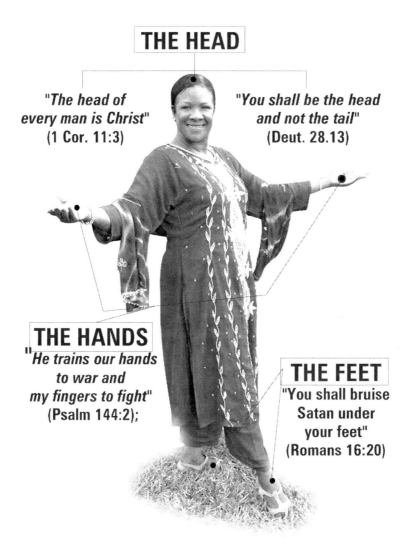

THE HEAD

"The head of every man is Christ" (1 Cor. 11:3)

"You shall be the head and not the tail" (Deut. 28.13)

THE HANDS

"*He trains our hands to war and my fingers to fight*" (Psalm 144:2);

THE FEET

"You shall bruise Satan under your feet" (Romans 16:20)

As we watched in amazement, we began to copy some of the movements and to dance right where we were, and to sing praises to the Lord about His goodness. The tour around the aquarium brought such an anointing on us that when we left, driving all the way home we praised, prayed, cried and sang unto our God for allowing us to see a part of His creation which showed forth His glory.

God always intended for His creation to be creative. When we are creative we begin to show forth His glory or His nature. When you dance you are creating expressions of His glory. An un-regenerated man can only show forth the nature of the fallen man; the regenerated man shows off the nature of God, because he is born of the Spirit of God.

PRAISE DANCE

There is Praise unto the Lord in Dance. We begin to joyously express to God, about God, in forms of movement that causes us to Leap up or Spring forth which is the meaning of the Greek word Exallomai. Praise will exalt or honor your God as you boast about Him. Psalms 113 through Psalms 118 are called the Hallel. These are the Psalms that will cause you to praise God with all your might. Psalms 114 verse 4 says the mountains skipped like rams, and the little hills like lambs. The word skipped in that verse means to dance. Skirtao means to jump sympathetically, move, or leap for joy (Acts 3:4 and Acts 14:10).

When we are in a praise service, we should begin to sing and dance with joy in our hearts unto the King of kings because of who He is and what He has done on Calvary for us. God commands us to enter into His gates with thanksgiving. As a dancer, your duty in service is to encourage those that are outside of the gates to enter in joyfully, leaving all of their problems behind them, and by faith begin to thank God for what He has already done, what He is doing now, and what He will do in the future. As you begin to dance and move about throughout the congregation taking hold of a brother's or sister's hand encouraging them to enter in the gates of the Lord. As you run through the gates leaping and jumping, twirling and skipping, you will approach the courts of the Lord. As you see Him in the distance, you will then begin to praise Him and show forth your expression of how you feel about Him, telling Him how wonderful and glorious He is and how excellent His name is in all the earth. That is when we become clamorously foolish like David did in II Samuel 6:16, for that is the moment when God shows up, when you get foolish over Him. David danced with all of his might, with everything that was in him-his spirit, soul and body-when he began to praise his God. When we dance with such fervency showing off how we feel about our God, then it will cause others to desire the same relationship. There may be those who despise you and not understand the relationship between you and the Father, as Michal despised David because she did not understand how David felt about his God. Remember, not every one will feel the same way you feel about your God. Only you know what He has done and what He has brought you through. When I think of His goodness, His mercy and what He has done for me, all I can do is dance, dance, dance. Praise turns your mourning into dancing (Psalm 30:11-12).

WORSHIP DANCE

When you worship God with expressions of dance you have to lay yourself down and take on the spirit of Christ's life. Worship begins at the place of humility so that Christ can be seen in our dance.

Worship does not start with the hands and feet; worship begins with the heart and moves through our hands and feet and ends on our knees. It is loving the Lord with your whole heart, your soul and your might. Mary showed a demonstration of her love for Jesus as she moved into a different position: an attitude to reverence to Him. She bowed, then she kissed His feet, she anointed Him and she preserved His life so she could have her life preserved.

As we begin to surrender all that we are to Him with expressions of worship in movements that demonstrate an attitude of a spirit surrendered, soul submitted, and flesh crucified, then and only then can God be glorified. A worship dance should show intimacy between you and the Father. When you dance, people should be able to see that you only have one partner that you are dancing with, and that is the Holy Spirit. You should be dancing a slow dance that causes you to hold Him so close that no one can get in between you and your Partner, the Holy Spirit. You then become one like Jesus and the Father are one. This is how the oil then begins to flow from your head all the way down to your garment. You then begin to dance the dance you see the Father dance, following His footsteps every step of the way. Now even the hem of your garment as it flows when you dance can touch people and bring healing and deliverance.

The woman with the issue of blood reached out and touched the hem of Jesus' garment and she was healed (Luke 8:44). That same Christ, the Anointed One, lives on the inside of you. Intimacy in worship causes you to hear the voice of your Father and the voice of a stranger you will not follow nor obey (John 10: 4-5). As you dance, the Father will then speak to your heart and give you directions, telling you what steps to take and what moves to make that pleases Him.

Remember, your dance is unto the Lord, not unto man. Our dance should bring such great conviction that it draws man to God. It's the true nature of God that should be displayed through our dance because that is the real you, that's who He is seeking to worship Him. You are a spirit living in a body. God is not seeking your body to worship Him, but your spirit. John 4:23 says:

"But the hour cometh, and now is, when the true worshippers shall worship the Father in spirit and in truth: for the Father seeketh such to worship Him."

Worship is an attitude expressed, so when we dance, whatever our attitude is, it will be expressed, whether it's a good attitude or a bad one. God is looking for pure hearts and those with clean hands who have not lifted up their soul to vanity nor sworn deceitfully (Psalm 24: 3-4). This is the only way you will be able to enter into His holy place and have an intimate relationship with Him.

FESTIVAL DANCING

There are a number of feasts and holy days found in the book of Leviticus chapter 23. The Feast of Weeks which is one of the feasts celebrated, is the time when you show thanksgiving for the Lord's blessing of harvest. During this time there should be a procession of worshippers with their first-fruits of the wheat harvest giving willingly and cheerfully to the Lord of the harvest. The Feast of Weeks came fifty days after the Feast of Unleavened Bread. This was called the Pentecost Harvest because of the number fifty which meant Pentecost.

The book of Acts chapter 2 verse 1 says when the day of Pentecost came they were all together in one place. When we come together in one place to do a work for the Lord, we must be on one accord, especially as a group of dancers. We must have our procession in order, making sure it represents what we want to express at that time. Your baskets should be filled with wheat and your dance should be a joyful dance filled with thanksgiving.

The Feast of Purim (Est. 9:18-20) and the Feast of Passover (Leviticus 23:5) are the feasts that remind God's people that He is a deliverer. God used Esther to deliver His people nationally and He took the Israelites out of Egypt. This festival dance should portray a time of rejoicing, giving and sharing.

There are many other feasts and sacred days such as the Feast of Tabernacles (Lev. 23:33); Feast of the Unleavened Bread (Lev. 23:6-8); Day of Atonement (Lev., 16: and 23:26) Sacred Assembly (Lev. 23:36); Year of Jubilee (Lev. 25:8-55); The Sabbath (Ex. 20:8-121) and the Sabbath Year (Ex. 23:10-11).

When planning a festival, always depict and portray the purpose of the celebration. Priestly garments were a part of the celebrations along with unleavened bread, oil, flour, wine, gifts, freewill offerings, burnt offerings, grain offerings and offerings made by fire.

PROPHETIC INTERPRETATION THROUGH THE DANCE

I first experienced the move of the prophetic in dance in 1986. Pastor Judson Cornwall was a visiting minister at our Fellowship in Nassau, Bahamas. He was teaching on worship. He began to teach on the worthiness of God and His sovereignty. At the end of the teaching he asked the congregation to stand and begin to worship the Lord. As I began to worship the Lord I began to feel His awesome presence. As His presence began to engulf me, I found myself moving from where I was standing and my body began to bend in different positions as I moved out into the midst of the congregation in rhythmic movements. I was singing a song of prophetic utterance. That went on for about two or three minutes, then one of the singers from the worship team began to interpret what the demonstration meant. At that moment my pastor, Dr. Myles Munroe, began to explain to the congregation what had just taken place and he said to them, "This is the beginning of more of the spiritual gifts being exercised in the church."

We see an example of the Prophetic Dance in Exodus 15 verses 20 and 21. After calling the women out with timbrels and dance, Miriam began to sing and dance, for the Lord, He hath triumphed gloriously, the horse and the rider hath He thrown into the sea.

When Israel defeated the Philistines and David had killed Goliath, the returning army was greeted with songs and dance. (Saul has slain his thousand and David his tens of thousands).

There were Old Testament prophets, spokesmen for God who would speak what God instructed them to. There were true and false prophets (Jer. 28:9).

The prophetess is a woman who exercises the prophetic gift of God. There were several women in the Bible known for this: Miriam, the sister of Moses (Exodus 15:20); Deborah (Judges 4:4); Huldah (II Kings 22:14); and the wife of Isaiah who bore him children with prophetic names (Isa. 8: 3). In the New Testament Philip the evangelist had four daughters who were unmarried, but also operated in the prophetic gift (Acts 2 l; 8-9).

DANCE OF WAR

Warfare in the dance is birthed out of prayer and intercession. It is called the Dance of Travail. This dance involves movements of the hand and feet with power and strength. 2 Cor. 10:4 says that:

> **"… the weapons of our warfare are not carnal but mighty through God to the pulling down of strongholds."**

In the book of Ephesians 6:12 it says:

> **"… we do not wrestle against flesh and blood but against principalities and powers, against the rulers of the darkness of this world, against wicked spirits in high places."**

Sometimes I would be awakened by the Holy Spirit in the early hours of the morning to pray and intercede for someone and I would be like a mighty warrior, dancing and pulling down strongholds.

If anyone saw me they would think I was fighting with someone in the natural. Whatever goes on in the supernatural realm will manifest itself in the natural. At those moments of intense intercession, it is God who will teach your hands how to war and your fingers how to fight (Psalm 144:1).

The dance of war can be done with a group of dancers standing in a circle, starting with one person in the middle letting her or his request be made known. Then the dancers may begin to use their hands to pull down whatever the spirit is, for example, the person may be struggling with the spirit of oppression. So they would pull down, then begin to trample it under their feet, dance on it and then jump and shout for the victory. There can be other demonstrations led by the Holy Spirit. He can give you other instructions as what to do. (Study the chapters on the dancers hands and feet).

PROCESSIONALS

Processionals are groups of persons moving along in an orderly form. In most processions in religious organizations you would find persons marching with banners bearing signs and symbols representing the King of Kings, The Lamb of God, The Mighty One of Israel, etc. Jehovah Nissi is the Lord our Banner.

Banners rally the troops in war. They also bestow honor to our God. Banners can be used in processionals to show forth the glory and splendor of God. Psalm 60: 4 tells us God has given a banner to them that fear thee, that it may be displayed because of the truth. And in Exodus 17:15 we are to lift up the Lord, for He is our banner, Jehovah-Nissi.

In most processions the singers, musicians and dancers lead, while the rest of the worshippers follow with banners and flags proclaiming the Lordship of Jesus Christ the King of kings. This is a time of celebration and proclamation. Most processions are done during the beginning of a church conference to declare the Lordship and authority of Jesus over the service from the very beginning. Children, youths and adults all participate together joining in unity to worship the King of kings. Psalm 133 talks about how good and pleasant it is for brethren to dwell together in unity … For it is there that the Lord commands the blessings and life over us.

Processions are done very often here in the Bahamas. When there is a funeral, different groups from various organizations participate by marching and playing different kind of instruments like horns, flutes, drums as well as the blowing of whistles. Although the occasion may be a sad one, rejoicing and praises still go up to the Lord for His goodness toward that person, and on many occasions there are individuals who give their life to the Lord during the funeral, or as we call it here in The Bahamas, a home-going.

Processionals are done during church anniversary celebrations also. There is a processional during the month of July which is called the Glory of Youth Month. All of the youths of our nation take to the streets and they praise and worship God with their instruments and sing and dance, lifting banners high which proclaim the Lordship of Jesus Christ.

REVIEW OF CHAPTER 1

1. Who created movement? _____ .

2. Who moved upon the face of the waters? _____

   _____

3. When God put man together, He made the body in a way that man

   can be _____ and _____ .

4. List two scriptures which states that we are to praise God in the dance

   a. _____

   b. _____

5. What is the meaning of the Hebrew word karar?

   _____

   _____

6. What is one of the positions of the act of worship?

   _____

GOD IS A GOD OF MOVEMENT

7. List four categories of dance:

    a. _____

    b. _____

    c. _____

    d. _____

8. What is warfare dance birthed out of?

    _____ and _____

9. True or false (Write 'T' for true and 'F' for false):

    _____ Skirtao (Greek) means to be sober, still and quiet before the Lord.

    _____ God commands us to enter into His gates with thanksgiving.

    _____ Worship begins with the heart.

    _____ One of the Old Testament Feasts is called the Feast of Purity.

    _____ The weapons of our warfare are mighty through God.

    _____ Even the mountains and the hills praise God.

    _____ The woman with the issue of blood reached out and touched Jesus' sleeves.

CHAPTER 2

PRESERVING THE BODY THROUGH MOVEMENT

Matthew 9:1-6

"Jesus spoke to the man sick of the palsy lying on the bed and said "Son, be of good cheer, thy sins be forgiven thee."

In verse 6 Jesus said: "Arise, take up thy bed and go unto thine house." In order for that man to be healed he had to move beyond his faith and put it into action. Jesus saw his faith, but then the man had to move. He had to take a step further and get up or arise to a standing position instead of lying down.

Jesus first said to the man, "your sins are forgiven," because sin will keep us bound to the guilt that will cause us not to move. We will become immobilized. Sin will cripple you. First you will have to receive forgiveness, and when you believe that God has forgiven you, then freedom and liberty takes place and that which once bound you, becomes loosed. The guilt of sins disappears and it causes you to rise up from a laid-down position. Jesus knew He had the power to forgive sins. He knew that it was easier to be forgiven than taking up the bed was going to be.

Also in the same chapter, verses 24 and 25, the young maiden laid there. They said she was dead, but Jesus said she was asleep. They laughed him to scorn. He went in, took her by the hand and the maiden arose. She moved, she got up from her original state. (Also found in Luke 8: 49-56).

15

LUKE 8:43-48

The woman who had the issue of blood had to move from where she was to touch Jesus. It took the reaching out of her hand, and then she had to go really low to get to the hem. She went a step further and fell on her knees; she moved from one position to another to get her healing. She then moved to the position of being preserved. This woman's faith and desperation caused her to move further than she had been moving before.

In Mark 6:53-56 when Jesus came to the land of Gennasaret, everyone knew Him. They ran, moved through the whole region round about. They began to carry in beds, those who were sick to where He was. They were determined to reach Jesus, even if they could just touch His garments.

These people saw it necessary to move from where they were in order to be healed, so they did what was necessary, they ran to where they needed to be in order to preserve their body.

LUKE 7: 37

A woman in the city was a sinner. She knew that Jesus was in the Pharisee's house. She had to move in order to get her alabaster box of ointment to Jesus. She stood behind Jesus, then bent down at His feet, began to weep, then took her hands and began to wash his feet with her tears and wipe His feet with her hair.

1. First, she got up from where she was. She moved.

2. Second, she went to a place of positioning—she stood behind Jesus: a place of submission to the authority to who He is.

3. She went into action—she began to wash His feet with her tears.

4. Then she wiped them with her hair—she completed the washing by wiping. She did not stop in the middle of her assignment, considering what others might say.

5. She kissed His feet—showing value or worth to who He is and what He meant to her, bowing to the lowest part of the body and giving reference and value, for the feet are also a position of authority. The feet are what will tread on serpents and scorpions and the powers of the air.

6. The feet were then anointed. She preserved the authority. She put that which was valuable on the feet because she knew the value or worth of the One whom she was anointing. She knew that He was the Anointed One who could preserve her life and destroy the yoke of bondage from her life. It was her movement that preserved her life or it was her making a decision to move that preserved her life. This woman whose sins had been much, had been forgiven much because she had loved much.

JOHN 5

There was a certain man who had an infirmity for thirty years. Jesus asked the man if he desired to be healed. In verse 7 the man told Jesus he had no man to put him into the pool, but Jesus said, "Arise, take up your bed and walk." Immediately the man was made whole, took up his bed and walked and it was on the Sabbath day. If the man did not move, he would not have been healed.

He could have missed his healing because:

1. He refused to move from the state he was in.

2. He was waiting on someone to change his situation.

3. He was blaming his condition on the excuse of not having help from others. He did not really believe that it took his faith and action to move him from the bed to the pool.

4. He allowed discouragement to keep him out of the pool. Those who was desperate all moved in front of him. He needed to be just as desperate as the others.

Jesus showed him how easy it was. Jesus spoke and he responded, despite it being on a day when the Jews felt that you should not be healed. He got up, he moved, he made a decision not to be in the same position anymore. That was when his condition changed. Authority spoke to him and he was preserved through him obeying by moving. Movement preserved his life.

It is in Christ we live and move and have our being.

JOHN 1: 44

Lazarus of Bethany was Mary's brother. The same woman who anointed Jesus' feet; the one who got her life preserved through Jesus. She was now in mourning and trying to help someone else's life to be preserved who was now dead. When Jesus heard of Lazarus, He spoke what He wanted, not what He had heard. He heard that Lazarus was dead, but He said, "I will awaken him from his sleep." Then Jesus explained to them that Lazarus was dead but His faith said that Lazarus was only asleep. Lazarus had been in the grave for four days at that time.

1. He remained in a state with no movement for four days.

2. There was more unbelief spoken than words of faith. They spoke death and Jesus spoke life saying in verse 23, "Thy brother shall rise again."

3. Jesus commanded them to take away the stone.

4. Then Jesus spoke to Lazarus himself and said, "Lazarus, come forth," (verses 43, 44). Lazarus was bound with a napkin, but Jesus said unto them, "Loose him and let him go."

5. Lazarus was able to move his hands, feet, and body, so that he could be alive and preserved.

Some of us are dead because we refuse to move all the parts of our body that was given to us. To move the body is to have circulation of life flowing through it.

ACTS 3: 1-19

There was a certain man lame from birth. Everywhere he needed to go he had to be carried. Peter and John were going into the temple and the man was begging for alms.

Peter said, "Look on us."

He was saying to the man to focus or listen. "Silver and gold have I none; but such as I have I give unto thee," (this was the anointing to destroy the yoke of bondage).

They said, "in the name of Jesus Christ, arise, get up and walk."

He took him by the right hand and lifted him up, and immediately his feet and anklebones received strength. Soon he was jumping and leaping (or dancing) and praising God. All the people saw him dancing and praising God and were amazed.

1. The man listened to Peter and John.

2. He obeyed them and got up from his position.

3. His body responded to his faith through obedience.

4. He began to dance and praise God after he received his healing from God.

5. He showed others his faith when he got healed. They knew of his condition from birth.

6. The disciples were able to testify of the Christ whom the people did not believe in, and told the people to repent, for it was this Christ the whom man believed in, that made him whole—THE ANOINTED ONE.

REVIEW OF CHAPTER 2

1. In order for the man sick of the palsy to be healed, he had to _____

_____.

2. What has a crippling effect on man? _____

3. List some reasons why the man by the pool who had an infirmity for thirty years could have missed out on his healing?

_____

_____

_____

_____

_____

CHAPTER 3

THE PROPHETIC DANCE ...

DANCING WITH A PURPOSE

I travel around the world from country to country, state to state, and everywhere I go, each engagement is a different experience. I remember when the mantle of the prophetic dance fell upon me. I was in Milwaukee, Wisconsin at Pastor Andréa Dudley's church. She had invited me to speak and to minister in dance. It was a Sunday morning service which was the end of the weeklong seminar, I was asked to minister in dance. The music I used was a song called, "The Potter's House" by Tramaine Hawkins.

Before dancing, the Lord had me minister to people by speaking to those who were broken in their marriage, single life, emotions or whatever situations in their lives that may have been turned upside down. After encouraging them, I began to dance and about the middle of the song I began to hear God speak to me. He instructed me to move into the aisle of the church and begin to dance around the people. I obeyed the Lord, then I began to stop by individuals whom the Lord had pointed out to me and I would prophesy to them then continue to dance.

God had told me to pull certain individuals into the aisles and just dance around them. The power of God was so strong that they could not stand on their feet. I began to dance and as I turned, my garment would touch someone and they would fall under the power of God. After the meeting many shared their experiences of how God healed them. The meeting went on for almost forty-five minutes while the music team continued to play and sing after the track had stopped. That day the scheduled speaker never got to speak because God had spoken through the dance.

The Pastor had given permission for the ministry to continue, so under his authority, I was able to continue dancing and ministering to the people.

The purpose of the dance is so that God would be glorified. His desire is to use our gifts and talents to draw people to Christ and also so that they will recognize His sovereignty. We are to be the evidence of His ability to heal, deliver and set people free from the hand of the enemy.

THE PROPHETIC DANCE

None of this would have been possible if I had not been in the Lord's presence seeking Him for what He desired to take place in that meeting. We have the gift of dancing but we must remember that Jesus is the giver of the gift. There is a price for His presence and it is called sacrifice. When we sacrifice our will we get God's will on earth as it is in the heavens. When you dance in the presence of God then it will attract the lost, the sick, the depressed, the down-trodden and oppressed.

During this time of ministry, moving in the prophetic through the dance, the Lord began to change the type of garments I would wear for that season. Because the movement of the prophetic dance is so much different from the flow of praise dance, worship or processional dancing, our garments have to best suit our movements. The prophetic dance is the voice of God in action. Have you ever watched someone talking and suddenly their hands are moving as they speak? All of their body is now in motion, because words were not enough to relate the message so that it could be clearly understood. The prophetic dance becomes the active manifestation of God's presence. The prophetic dance is birthed during the sixth level of praise Barak (baw-rak) {Hebrew}. It's when we become silent and wait on God. This is when we kneel in adoration before God. The psalmist David said, "Oh come let us worship and bow down," (Ps. 95:6 KJV). Then it is manifested during Tehillah. This is when God begins to respond to man. God begins to inhabit our praises of triumph (1 Chronicles 16:35).

Because God is God all by Himself, He can choose to manifest Himself or His glory, which is His nature, through any of the gifts He has imparted to man. It is His treasure that was put in earthen vessels so that He may reveal Himself. During this time of waiting on the Lord, there could be a song of the Lord or a word of the Lord.

1 Corinthians 14:15 says:

"I will pray with my spirit, but I will also pray with my mind; I will sing with my spirit, but I will sing with my mind.

This is where the demonstration of the prophetic takes place also. We see in 2 Chronicles 20: 22 that:

"... when they began to sing and to praise, the Lord set ambushments against the people of Ammon, Moab, and Mount Seir, who had come against Judah: and they were defeated."

Also in the book of Isaiah 42:10-12 it is written:

> **"Sing to the Lord a new song and His praise from the end of the earth, you who go down to the sea and all that is in it, you coastlands and you inhabitants of them. (11) Let the wilderness and its cities lift up their voice. The villages that Kedar inhabits let the inhabitants of Seal sing. Let them shout from the top of the mountains. (12) Let them give glory to the Lord and declare His praises in the coastlands."**

DANCING WITH A PURPOSE

As the level of anointing increases in my life the responsibilities increase and that requires spending even more time with God. When I would return home from traveling the first morning I wake up I would run to the beach and begin jogging. My home is only a block away from the beautiful blue waters which calls to me when I'm home. My meeting place with the Lord has always been the beach. As I jog I talk to Him and He talks back to me. He gives me songs to sing to Him. So you see, my special moments are spending time with God. That is how I get directions from Him for my life.

I knew that the dance had a purpose beyond Praise & Worship during a Sunday morning service. I believe, as I have experienced the move of God in such powerful ways, so many times, in so many services around the world, that the dance ought to bring healing, deliverance and salvation to souls. When we don't know the purpose of dance we can abuse it, then unbelievers, as well as believers, can become confused as to what the purpose of dance is in the church.

One day I sat on a flight to Ft. Lauderdale on my way to Dallas, Texas for a week-long conference. We were delayed for 1 hour because of the weather, and they had already given us the bad news stating that it was going to be a bumpy flight and that we will be even further delayed. I began to speak to God and said, "God, the air waves belong to You. Clear the clouds, part them like you parted the Red Sea so the plane can go through smoothly. Show me a sign of Your goodness. In Ps. 86: 17, You promised to help me and comfort me." As the plane lifted, the dark clouds parted and we burst forth into brilliant sunshine. The Pilot then spoke and said, "We are now out of Nassau and we will be having a smooth ride from here on." I then began to thank God and smile as I heard the pilot talking over the system. The scripture says: "The angel of the Lord encamps about those who fears Him." (Ps. 34: 7)

When God has a purpose for your life, then purpose preserves life. If God has called you to minister in the area of dance, then use your gifts to bring souls into the kingdom of God. People should be uplifted and encouraged after you have ministered in the presence of the Lord and in the midst of the people. I had purpose to be fulfilled in Dallas so God preserved me so I could get there to fulfill it. I was born with a purpose and that purpose is: "I was Born To Dance!" God has ordained my steps to dance in many places and it takes cars, trains and planes to get me there, therefore, God will protect me and sustain me. He loves me this I know and believe. He always tells me, "Ann I love you, I'll do anything for you," and I'll do anything for my Lord. When the Lord puts a call on your life, and gives you a gift, it is for a purpose.

You must know the purpose of the dance is to advance the Kingdom of God. When Herod's daughter danced, she danced with a purpose, a purpose to please the King enough so that she could get what she wanted from him, which was John the Baptist's head (Mark 6:26).

My Pastor did a teaching at one of our dance conferences on "Why We Dance". That was the day I got the revelation of the fore-mentioned scripture. The Lord spoke to me that night and said, "Ann I want you to see that when the daughter of Herodias danced for Herod and his guest," He said, "she pleased them, or rather, brought pleasure to them to such a degree that he swore an oath to give her whatever she requested, up to half of his kingdom." Then the Lord said, "You have a King of all kings that you can dance before, and when you please the King He hands out His scepter to you to enter into His presence." He said, "I created Herod who was a king, his guest and the girl." "The earth is mine and the fullness of it and all they that dwell within it. You can ask and receive whatsoever you need." The need may be deliverance for loved ones, salvation, or healing, He is a God that is more than enough. He then spoke to me and said, "When you dance, be sure your desire becomes My desire," and I said, "Lord, what do you mean?" and He said, "My desire is that no man perish but they all come to repentance and have everlasting life." (2 Peter 3:9) "My desire is for men be healed, delivered and set free from the hand of the enemy." "As you dance, you must see Me healing people, setting them free from the bondage of the enemy, then because you would have sought my kingdom first, I will begin to add every thing you have need of and you would not have to worry about your personal needs (Matt. 6:33). God's one desire is that we please Him and only Him, then we will be in perfect peace. When a man's ways please God He makes even his enemy's to be at peace with him (Prov. 16:7). We must remember that we are sons and daughters of the most high God.

John the Baptist was a prophet who not only lost his head because a dancer pleased the king, but his whole ministry was totally destroyed. Her dance was used for evil, but could you imagine if we dance to please our King? It is His good pleasure to give us the kingdom (Luke 12:32).

When you dance you give life or death. There are dancers when they dance you have to close your eyes or you will lose your head because their spirit is not fully committed to the Lord. Your heart must be fully committed to the Lord your God to live by His decrees and obey His commands (1 Kings 8:61).

My pastor told me that when God told him I was going to dance for the kingdom of God he said he had never seen dance in the church, he did not know what it looked like. Then God said to him, "The only gift she has is dance, so let her use it." That is why we have to let the gifts of the body of Christ come out. God gave us many talents, but He also gave us a gift to reveal His glory.

Many times people ask, "Why do we dance?" It is part of the worship experience. God created everything, so everything that exists belong to God. God created the dance but Satan perverted it; because he was perverted he transferred perversion to everything he touched. Your hands that clap belong to God; your feet that dance belong to God; your body that moves belongs to God. You can use these instruments for the glory of God or you can work against the work of the Lord. Jesus came to destroy the works of the devil, therefore, He has given us power and authority over all devils and to cure diseases just as He had given to His disciples, for we are the disciples of the Lord (Luke 9:1).

We see in the book of Exodus 15 Miriam leading an entire congregation into dancing and the Pastor (Moses) wrote the song they danced to. Therefore Pastors should have no problem with a dancing congregation. The church was so large that Miriam had to find a large stage so she had to use the desert.

When we assemble ourselves together as God commands us, there are seven levels of praise that God commands us to take when we approach Him. In each expression we find ourselves using a member of our body. TOWDAH (to-daw) {Hebrew} is the first dimension of praise. It means to lift your hands and extend thanks to the Lord. Psalms 100: 4 tells us to:

"... enter into His gates with thanksgiving and into His courts with praise: be thankful unto Him and bless His name."

So as we worship the Lord we express our praise to Him with our hands in motion, dancing before the lord. This is a sacrifice of the will because we don't care who is watching us, we don't care if we feel like it or not, but we are willing to offer God a sacrifice. Psalm 26:7 says:

"That I may proclaim with the voice of thanksgiving and tell of all Your wondrous works."

This sacrifice takes us right into the second level of praise: YADAH, which is another dimension. You entered into the gates with thanksgiving, which is TOWDAH, now you have arrived into the courts with praise which is YADAH. The dancer's role in the congregation is to take the hands of their fellow brother or sister and get them into the gates and courts of the Lord. Many times we find that people come to church depressed, sick, or just tired and the enemy uses our mind as the battle ground, especially when we come to worship the Lord. We think about whether we left the stove on at home, or our son who is on drugs who did not come home last night and wonder if he is alright. We are to help them get their minds on Christ, so as we are dancing, we may take ahold of their hand and invite them to praise the Lord. When you start praising God you don't have time to think of anything other than His goodness.

Now we come to the third level of praise: HALAL. It's a primary root word which our word hallelujah comes from. When you think of God's faithfulness towards you and His mercies which are new every morning, you then begin to act like David did: clamorously foolish. Sometimes I wish I had more hands and feet to praise and dance before the Lord with so I can express to Him how much I love and appreciate Him.

Now as we begin to tell God how awesome and majestic His name is in all the earth, this is called SHABACH, which is the fourth level. This is where you can get a good shout to the Lord. Psalm 47:1 says:

"Shout to the Lord with a voice of triumph."

ZAMAR is the fifth level. Psalms 150:3-6 states that we are to:

"Praise Him with the sound of the trumpet; Praise Him with the lute and harp! (4) Praise Him with the timbrel and dance; Praise Him with stringed instruments and flutes! Praise Him with loud cymbals; Praise Him with clashing cymbals!"

When you dance you can appreciate the fifth level of praise because that's when the other gifts tap into God, with their instruments giving life to their praise. The music gives you a boost of energy that causes you to dance with all your soul and strength. This causes us to ascend to the hill of the Lord and we also get God's attention as well.

So now God is ready to respond to our call. We are to be silent and expect from God. He said if we call upon Him, He would answer us and show us great and mighty things we know not of (Jeremiah 33:3). It's like running up a high hill to meet your lover and you finally made it. And now you can finally rest in him. That is called BARAK (baw-rak) {Hebrew}. This is where we kneel in adoration before the Lord.

The seventh level is called TEHILLA. You are now in the presence of the Holy One. This is the praise God has been waiting for: utterances inspired by the Holy Ghost. In the first six levels of praise it is what we do, but in the seventh level it is what God does, and that is not predictable. This is the place God desires to dwell (Psalm 22:3). God is jealous and He doesn't share His praises with anyone or anything because He wants us to become His praise (Jeremiah 33:11). God desires intimacy with us during worship.

The dance comes in on the third level of praise. While dancing in the service at church we can either take people up to the hill of the Lord, or we can take them down hill. The dance is a command from the Lord (Psalms 149:3 and 150:4). We are to get His manifest presence into the church and the dance plays an important role in accomplishing this. We want to get into His presence but we want to do it our way instead of God's way, even if it means skipping a few levels to get there. This does not work.

God anoints the dancer like Miriam to lead the people into worship because dance is their gift. Not every one who dances is anointed to dance. It is very important that we seek the Lord as to what our calling is. If we are to reveal His glory through our gift then we are make sure we are in the right position, because His presence is our ultimate goal. We are filled with a power which is trapped inside of us waiting to be revealed. Ephesians 3:20 says

"Now unto Him who is able to do exceedingly abundantly above all that we ask or think according to the power that worketh in us."

The power is in us and God wants to get it out through the gifts, which can be singing, dancing, playing and instrument, etc. If you have lost the glory, which is the Holy Spirit, it's also God's presence. Jesus came and died so that you could have life again and the glory, which is His nature, can be restored back to you again. This glory cannot be manifested in us when we are lost in sin. The only place you can become who you are with your gift of dance is in His presence. This is how you will be able to reveal your true potential. His presence brings satisfaction and gratification. Then you will not find yourself moving from dance ministry to dance ministry, or from church to church. Our excuse is we are looking for God's presence, but God is saying, "You are the one to manifest My presence through My gift of dance." David said,

"Bless the Lord, oh my soul and all that is within me bless His holy name." (Psalm 103:1)

When you dance you are to bless the Lord with all that is within you. What is within you? The power and the ability of God.

SIN STOPS THE GLORY

What stops the glory? Sin stops the glory from being revealed. As a dancer we are to live pure lives before God. We must not let our good be spoken of as evil (Romans 14:16). When Adam sinned he lost the Holy Spirit, which is God's presence. When you lose the presence of God you cannot dance freely nor can the anointing flow through you. Dance, then, becomes sweat and hard work. Entertainers and performers work. Only grace keeps us alive when we know so many times we have come into the sanctuary and worship on the altar of the Lord with unclean hands, impure hearts and wrong motives. We sometimes have ought against other dancers in our group and because of pride we would not get it right. God hates sin. If we were living in the days of King David we would have been dead trying to touch His presence with sin in our lives. God's requirements is that we consecrate ourselves when we want to bring up the Ark (His presence) (1 Chron.15:12-14). God has given us the keys to the kingdom and the only way they will be able to unlock any door of the kingdom is when we lay our gifts on the altar and go and get it right with our brother or sister. If we walk in disobedience, our dance will bring death instead of life.

Sin keeps the hidden treasure from being exposed. We have a treasure in earthen vessels. God wants His hidden treasure that is in you, revealed. There are steps you have not danced yet that are hidden in you. And God is waiting to reveal it through you. God said you are the light of the world and He wants to put you on a hill where everyone can see you. Your dance should be known around the world. God wants to expose you to the world so His glory can be seen. Sin will clog up the line that causes His glory to flow. My Pastor, Dr. Myles Munroe, the presence of God this way: "The presence of God is the active manifestation of God that fills the atmosphere and environment in which creation dwells."

REVIEW OF CHAPTER 3

1. As a dancer, it is important to seek the _____ for what He desires in a meeting.

2. The prophetic dance is the _____ of God in _____.

3. The prophetic dance is birthed out of what level of praise? _____ (Hebrew).

4. As the level of anointing increases in your life, the responsibilities increase which requires spending _____ time with _____.

5. List seven levels of praise:

   _____   _____

   _____   _____

   _____   _____

   _____   (Hebrew words)

6. What will prevent the glory of God from flowing when you dance?

   _____

CHAPTER 4

THE ROYAL GARMENTS

The question always arises: "How do I dress to minister in the dance?"

Let me ask you, who are you dancing for? Is it for the people or is it for the King of kings? It is written in the Word that the earth is the Lord's and the fullness thereof, the world and those that dwell within (Psalm 24 v 1). If everything belongs to God, then whatever we bring before Him should be the best of what belongs to Him. When we prepare to dance before the king our garments should show forth the beauty of His holiness and His glory or should bring glory to Him. We are kings and priest in the earth. We are a royal priesthood. We see this in 1 Peter 2 v 5:

"You also, as living stones, are being built up a spiritual house, a holy priesthood, to offer up spiritual sacrifices acceptable to God through Jesus Christ."

In Exodus 28 v 1-4 when Aaron and his sons were chosen from among the children of Israel to minister unto the Lord as priests, they took them and made holy garments for them. They were for glory and beauty. They also chose people who were gifted in the area of the making of garments. Not any and every one were allowed to make their garments. When I danced in the casino as a lead dancer it was not holy, sanctified people who made my garments: G-strings and topless bras. But if I want someone to make my garment for worship I need to find someone who has the mind of God so that they will know the things of the Spirit.

Secondly, the persons assigned for this task were filled with the spirit of wisdom. These garments, along with Aaron, were consecrated unto the Lord, which means they had decided to dedicate their garments and themselves for service and worship unto the lord. Just as God called Aaron to minister unto Him as a priest, He has also called us to minister unto Him as priests.

Aaron and his sons also wore under garments to cover their nakedness. Read Exodus 28 v 42-43:

"And you shall make for them linen trousers to cover their nakedness; they shall reach from the waist to the thighs. (43) They shall be on Aaron and on his sons when they come into the tabernacle of meeting, or when they come near the altar to minister in the holy place, that they do not incur iniquity and die. It shall be a statute forever to him and his descendants after him."

So many dance ministries are cancelled because of them not being properly dressed. We have to realize that not every one in the sanctuary to whom you are ministering is saved or converted in their minds. We have to remember that God is concerned for souls and we do not want to cause a soul to be lost because of our ignorance.

Some of us are upset because our pastor has not accepted our ministry of dance in the church, but you never know what dancer or whose ministry he saw that made him say, "I do not want that to happen in my church." Many pastors have said to me that they never believed in dance in the church until they saw me minister in dance. They were blessed by my attire and they would invite me to start a dance ministry in their church. That is why the God gave precise instructions to the people who were making Aaron's and his sons' garments. You may say, "Well, that was for Aaron and his sons," but the Word says that it shall be a statute forever to him and his descendants after him, and we are the generation after him.

I have seen dancers minister under such a great anointing but because of their attire the ministry was poorly received. People spend more time looking at the dancer twirling and their garments rising above their waist with nothing but a pair of stockings on under their garments clinging to their bodies; or wearing leotards though having large sized busts and no support bra. This is sure to distract people's attention away from the message of the dance and on to yourself. This inappropriate choice of clothing may "turn off" some from receiving the dance as a ministry; or "turn on" some, if you know what I mean. We should wear clothing which is appropriate for dancing in the presence of the King of kings.

I believe that you should wear different types of garments to accompany your dance. If you are dancing to a worship song then your garment should express worship; the same applies to the prophetic, praise or processional dance.

I believe we should spend time preparing to go before our King. So many times I have had dancers calling me at the last minute before they were about to minister asking to borrow a dance dress, skirt, shoe or blouse. If you are a true priest in the area of dance then you will never be caught not being prepared or equipped for service unto the Lord. A surgeon will never go into surgery unprepared or a carpenter to work without his tools. How can you claim to be a dancer and have no dance attire. I do not encourage such behavior anymore. I encourage dancers to purchase what they don't have, so when the need comes up they will be well prepared. A person that is preparing to be married will not wait until the wedding day to go and look for a wedding dress unless she is not sure that the groom has called her to be his bride. Jesus said He is coming back for a bride that is ready, or prepared, without spot or wrinkle.

When you respect and reverence the Lord who is our King, you would not go before him dressed any kind of way. In verse 4 of Exodus 28 God was very detailed with the garments He told them to make for Aaron and his sons. He gave them designs and colors. Even the breastplate that they wore had the twelve stones on the front representing the twelve tribes of Judah. If you seek the Lord concerning what to wear and the colors to wear He will give it to you. You have to seek the face of God for His perfect will concerning your ministry. You will find divine favor from the King when you respect and reverence Him. Esther was a great example for us in preparation for service unto the King. She was highly favored and got what she wanted from the king because she knew how to approached him. She spent a lot of time in preparation, fasting and praying and seeking for directions. When you are about to minister unto the King, how much time do you spend seeking directions on what to wear or what song to minister to. How many times do you seek to know the order of the service through the mind of the Spirit so that the order of the service, which was given to the Pastor by the Lord and handed down to the music leader, would be caught by the musicians, singers, and dancers so that every one would flow in one accord to bring the glory in the temple. We can learn from Esther:

"Each young woman's turn came to go in to King Ahasuerus after she had completed twelve months' preparation, according to the regulations for the women, for thus were the days of their preparation apportioned: six months with oil of myrrh, and six months with perfumes and preparations for beautifying women. Thus prepared, each young woman went to the king, and she was given whatever she desired to take with her from the women's quarters to the king's palace." (Esther 2 v 12-13-NKJV)

The King expects a gift when you come before Him. God created us to be a gift to Him. He did not give us a gift to give back to Him; He owns everything. Why would God give you something just so that you could give it back to Him? No, He created us a treasure on earth to show forth His glory or nature through us. We can be that gift given back to Him after we have done well with the potential and purpose as to why He has put us into the earth. God has given us talents and abilities to exercise on the earth and what we do with it is our gift back to God.

"Now when the turn came for Esther the daughter of Abihail the uncle of Mordecai, who had taken her as his daughter, to go in to the king, she requested nothing but what Hegai the king's eunuch, the custodian of the women, advised. And Esther obtained favour in the sight of all who saw her. So Esther was taken to King Ahasuerus, into his royal palace, in the tenth month, which is the month of Tebeth, in the seventh year of his reign. The King loved Esther more than all the other women and she obtained grace and favour in his sight more than all the virgins; so he set the royal crown upon her head and made her Queen instead of Vashti. Then the King made a great feast, the Feast of Esther, for all his officials and servants; and he proclaimed a holiday in the provinces and gave gifts according to the generosity of a king. (Esther 2 v 15-18—NKJV)

CONSECRATE YOUR GARMENTS

So many times I have seen dancers ministering in the dance and shortly after they are somewhere else in the same garment. Garments that are consecrated for service to the Lord should only be used for that purpose. I have had dancers asking to borrow dance garments to go to dance at their school socials and they were not ministering songs unto the Lord. My answer would always be, "No." I would always have my dancers change immediately after ministry, even before they go out into the congregation. Ezekiel 44: 16-19 says:

"They shall enter into My sanctuary, and they shall come near My table to minister to Me, and they shall keep My charge. And it shall be, whenever they enter the gates of the inner court, that they shall put on linen garments; no wool shall come upon them, while they minister within the gates of the inner court or within the house. They shall have linen turbans upon their heads and linen trousers on their bodies; they shall not clothe themselves with anything that causes sweat. When they go out to the outer court, to the outer court to the people, they shall take off their garments in which they have ministered, leave them in the holy chambers, and put on other garments; and in their holy garments they shall not sanctify the people. (NKJV)

SCRIPTURE REFERENCES ON GARMENTS
PURITY, MATURITY AND AUTHORITY:

(Luke 24 v 4) "And it happened as they were greatly perplexed about this that behold two men stood in shining garments."

IM-MATURITY, COVETING WHAT GOD HAD SPECIFIED FOR HIMSELF:

(Joshua 7 v 21) "When I saw among the spoils a beautiful Babylonian garment, two hundred shekels of silver, and a wedge of gold weighing fifty shekels, I coveted them and took them. And there they are, hidden in the earth in the midst of my tent, with the silver under it."

MOVING IN IGNORANCE AND CRAFTINESS:

(Joshua 9 v 4-5) "They worked craftily, and went and pretended to be ambassadors. And they took old sacks on their donkeys, old wine skins torn and mended, old and patched sandals on their feet, and old garments on themselves; and all the bread of their provision was dry and moldy."

MOVING IN WISDOM

(Ecclesiastes 9 v 8) "Let your garments always be white and let your head lack no oil."

WALKING IN THE FLESH:

(Jude 1:22-23) "And on some have compassion, making a distinction; but others save with fear, pulling them out of the fire, hating even the garment defiled by the flesh."

WALKING IN HOLINESS

(Revelation 3 v 4-5) "You have a few names even in Sardis who have not defiled their garments; and they shall walk with me in white, for they are worthy."

WALKING IN THE ANOINTING:

(Luke 8 v 43-44) "Now a woman, having a flow of blood for twelve years, who had spent all her livelihood on physicians and could not be healed by any, came from behind and touched the border of His [Jesus'] garment. And immediately her flow of blood stopped.

GARMENT OF BEAUTY:

(Isaiah 52 v 1) "Awake, Awake! Put on your strength, O Zion; put on your beautiful garments, O Jerusalem, the holy city! For the uncircumcised and the unclean shall no longer come to you."

GARMENT OF HEAVINESS:

(Isaiah 61 v 3) "To console those who mourn in Zion, to give them beauty for ashes, the oil of joy for mourning, the garment of praise for the spirit of heaviness; that they may be called trees of righteousness, the planting of the Lord, that He may be glorified."

CLOTH & COLORS

I believe that when we make our garments we should pray about the types of cloth and the colors. Some people are anointed in the area of choosing the right cloth and colors for certain types of garments. As I read about Lydia in the book of Acts, she was a woman of the cloth.

(Acts 16 v 13-15) "And on the Sabbath day we went out of the city to the riverside, where prayer was customarily made; and we sat down and spoke to the women who met there. Now a certain woman named Lydia heard us. She was a seller of purple from the city of Thyatira who worshipped God. The Lord opened her heart to heed the things spoken by Paul. And when she and her household were baptized, she begged us, saying, 'if you have judged me to be faithful to the Lord, come to my house and stay.' So she persuaded us."

Lydia was a wealthy and influential businesswoman. She sold cloth dyed purple. The colour purple exemplifies royalty. I believe Lydia was successful as a result of her prayer life; she was a worshipper. It's always a blessing to find successful merchants with great knowledge in materials and types of cloths as well as Spirit-filled and full of God's wisdom. I have met a few people with these qualifications: I respect the ministry of Lora Allison, who wrote the book called "Celebration" which was given to me by my pastor at the beginning of my ministry. I read her book and saw the pictures of her garments and said to myself, "That is how I would like to dress to dance before my King." She became a mentor to me in the area of garments through her book.

I began to seek the Lord, asking Him what to wear and how to make my garments for the different songs I would minister to. When I danced to "We Shall Behold Him" I wanted to dress like a bride; when I danced to "The Potter's House" I wanted to look like a broken vessel being mended. I wanted my garments to represent what I was portraying about the Lord. I was very precise in the materials I used. The silver represented 'redemption' and I had on a silver, sequined breastplate across the chest of my garment for that particular number.

I also have great respect for Joann Rush and Freda Cox who represent the kingdom of God in such excellence in their ministry. They would take materials and make the most beautiful garments fit for a King; they would have yards of silk cloth which they made into beautiful banners; the crowns that they made would have so many stones that you could tell they spent a lot of time seeking the Lord for ideas and asking Him to show them a glimpse of heaven so that they can duplicate it on earth. Joann and Freda, along with 'Flames of Fire', travel every year to the Bahamas to help organize an opening procession for the CCDN International Dance Conference. During the time of this procession the glory of the Lord fills the place and His presence causes people to be healed and delivered. Everything that is used creates an atmosphere for the King to show up.

Listed below you would find some of the colours used for garments, banners, flags etc., and what they represent:

RED .... The Blood

WHITE... Purity

GOLD... Divinity

PURPLE... Kingship, Royalty

GREEN .... Growth, Prosperity

BLUE ....Heavenlies, Dominion, Holy Spirit

SILVER...Redemption

YELLOW...Shekinah Glory

FUCHSIA ....Heart of Flesh

TURQUOISE .... Open Heaven

ORANGE .... Praise

IRIDESCENT.. Overcoming

REVIEW OF CHAPTER 4

1. Our garments should show forth the _____ of God's holiness and His _____ .

2. We are to the put on the garment of _____ against the spirit of heaviness.

3. We are to hate garments defiled by the _____ .

5. What do the colors listed below represent:

Purple _____

White _____

Red _____

Gold _____

4. True or false

____ Anyone should be allowed to make your dance garments.

____ We should always wear bra tops and fitting tights to dance unto the Lord.

____ We should consecrate our garments unto the Lord.

THE HANDS

*"He trains our hands
to war and
my fingers to fight"
(Psalm 144:2);*

CHAPTER 5

COMMANDMENTS CONCERNING THE HANDS

Zechariah 8:9

LET YOUR HANDS BE STRONG

In times of warfare and intercession a dancer must be strong, using the hand to pull down the strongholds of the enemy. The Holy Spirit is our Teacher, the One who helps you to fight the good fight of faith. He will teach your fingers to fight and your hands to war (Psalm 144 v 1). We are not to war against each other but we are to lift up each other and encourage each other to stay strong.

In times of praise, God will strengthen us when we continually lift our hands in waving movements and expressions as we continue to praise and worship the King.

Isaiah 35:3

'STRENGTHEN YE THE WEAK HANDS.'

We have to be strength to other dancers who may not have confidence in their ministry and are constantly buffeted by the devil through condemnation. God promised that He will be your strength in time of weakness. When the righteous run into God, he is safe.

Isaiah 52:11 (NIV)

'DEPART, DEPART GO OUT FROM THERE! TOUCH NO UNCLEAN THING! COME OUT FROM IT AND BE PURE, YOU WHO CARRY THE VESSELS OF THE LORD'

The Lord is saying to dancers, separate yourselves from the ways of the world. Whatever you set your hands to do must glorify God. Be not like them but be a light and an example to them. Once you become a dancer unto the Lord, you do not go back into the disco or the nightclub dancing unto the devil. God wants us to have a clean heart so that we can ascend into the hill of the Lord.

Numbers 16:26

'DEPART now FROM THE TENTS OF THESE WICKED MEN! TOUCH NOTHING OF THEIRS, LEST YOU BE CONSUMED IN THEIR SINS'

Sometimes as dancers, we are so easily influenced to perform for civic groups that are not into the presence of God, but who just want to be entertained. We must be careful about motivation. We are to be on an assignment when we go to minister anywhere. God will open doors and provide opportunities so we can go into the kingdom of darkness and proclaim the light of Jesus Christ.

HANDS USED BY, FOR AND OF GOD

a)   In Healing

Mark 16:18—'THEY SHALL LAY HANDS ON THE SICK ….'

Dancers' hands can flow with anointing as they minister in dance. Sometimes the Holy Spirit may minister to you to touch a person while you are dancing, and they can be healed. Even demons will flee as you lay your hands on the sick.

COMMANDMENTS CONCERNING THE HANDS

Acts 3:7—'AND HE TOOK HIM BY THE RIGHT HAND AND
LIFTED HIM UP, AND IMMEDIATELY HIS FEET AND ANKLE
BONES RECEIVED STRENGTH'

When ministering in the dance, the Holy Spirit may lead you to someone
who is lame or sick in his or her body. God causes the anointing to flow
out of your hands so that who ever you touch will receive a blessing from
God. Just reaching out in obedience will be a blessing, it is better than a
sacrifice.

b)   In Worship

Leviticus 7:30—'HIS OWN HANDS SHALL BRING THE OFFERING
OF THE LORD'

God is expecting you to bring an offering. That offering should be your
body, a vessel of honor fit for the master's use. As a priest unto the Lord, He
is expecting us to give Him pure offerings. Our dance is to be offered up to
the Lord, so every move we make will send up a sweet fragrance unto Him.
As we move into sacrificial praise, here are some scriptural movements:

Psalms 47:1—'Clap your hands all ye people'

Psalms 63:4—'I will lift up my hands in your name'

Psalms 119:48—'My hands also will I lift up'

As you follow these movements you will end up with a choreographed
dance.

c)   In Consecration

Psalms 119:109—'MY LIFE IS CONTINUALLY IN MY HAND, YET I
DO NOT FORGET YOUR LAW.'

Remember that your soul is only the servant, your body a slave, but the
spirit is king, and he is always ready to obey the law. The flesh always wants
to go its own way. Dancers are required to put their soul in the hands of the

49

Lord so that we will not walk after the flesh but only in the Spirit. We are to consecrate ourselves unto Him so He may be master over our flesh.

Luke 9:62—'BUT JESUS SAID TO HIM, NO ONE, HAVING PUT HIS HAND TO THE PLOW, AND LOOKING BACK, IS FIT FOR THE KINGDOM OF GOD.'

Our decision must be fixed on Christ, the Author and Finisher of our faith.

Our vision and goals must be Christ-centered. God is looking for dancers who are sold out and focused on the ultimate goal, which is souls. Everything we do must lead to salvation and deliverance.

1ST JOHN 1 V 1—'THAT WHICH WAS FROM THE BEGINNING, WHICH WE HAVE HEARD, WHICH WE HAVE SEEN WITH OUR EYES, WHICH WE HAVE LOOKED UPON, AND OUR HANDS HAVE HANDLED, CONCERNING THE WORD OF LIFE.'

We have felt the light of Christ, which is eternal life flowing through our fingertips as we flow and dance in the Spirit. We can testify of the goodness of God and His anointing. It is the same life of Jesus Christ which operates through us that bears witness of what we have seen and heard that others will know that there is life in Christ. So dance and let the life and light of Christ glow from you.

d)   In Witness

Luke 15:22—'… AND PUT A RING ON HIS HAND.'

We are the sons of the Most High God, brought out of darkness into His marvelous light. Having been brought back to our rightful position in Christ, we now bear witness, for he has put a robe of righteousness upon us and a ring on our finger. We are home to stay! We should never minister in dance under condemnation, but must be free in our spirits. As we dance it should show forth the freedom of Christ. Whom the Son has set free is free indeed.

e) For Guidance

Acts 9:8—'THEY LED HIM BY THE HAND.'

We should be guided by the Holy Spirit at all times. When we minister in the dance, our attitude should be "Holy Spirit, take me by the hand and lead me."

Don't put yourself in a position where God has to knock you down like Saul just to get you walking in your calling of dance. Be led by the Spirit of God in all your decisions.

f) For Giving

Proverbs 31:20—'SHE STRETCHETH OUT HER HAND TO THE POOR; YEA, SHE REACHETH FORTH HER HANDS TO THE NEEDY.' (KJV)

When we minister as dancers, our attitude should be that of giving. We are servants here to serve, give and share. Even our talent should be shared by teaching others who need help to learn about dance.

THE HANDS OF CHRIST

Mark 8 : 2 3—'HE TOOK THE BLIND MAN BY THE HAND AND LED HIM OUT OF THE TOWN.'

We represent Christ. When we put our hands on the blind, we put Christ's hands on the blind. The dance is just another tool which God has given us to bring healing to those who are blind to the gospel. There are many who are blind to the calling of the dance. Many, for that reason, reject this area of ministry, so be sure not to ever be a stumbling block in that area.

Luke 24:50—'AND HE LIFTED UP HIS HANDS AND BLESSED THEM.'

As disciples of the Lord, He has empowered us, so as a dance minister we can go out and cast out demons and heal the sick. That is why He lifted up His hands and blessed you to go out and make other disciples.

THE HANDS OF GOD

Exodus 13:3—'FOR BY STRENGTH OF HAND THE LORD BROUGHT YOU OUT OF THIS PLACE.'

Remember the hand of the Lord brought us up out of Egypt. We are now free! You cannot be bound and try to set others free. Your dance should show freedom.

Job 1 9 : 2 1—'THE HAND OF GOD HATH TOUCHED ME.'

If God had not touched you with His loving hands and reached out with His tender mercies, where would be today? His touch is what made you whole. His touch took your broken vessel and mended it again. His touch is what turned your mourning into dancing.

Job 12:10—'In whose hand is every living thing and the breath of all mankind.'

Thank God that every living thing is truly in God's hand. When you dance, it is God who changes the heart of every man. Do not look at their faces, just dance in spite of what you see in the natural. God will touch their heart.

1 Peter 5:6—'HUMBLE YOURSELF UNDER THE MIGHTY HANDS OF GOD'

Only when we humble ourselves will God exalt us in due time.

COMMANDMENTS CONCERNING THE HANDS

The spirit of humility is what Jesus had and His desire is for you to walk in that manner as a dance minister. Just be faithful over the little and He will make you ruler over much. Promotion is from above.

HANDS THAT REACHED OUT FOR JESUS

Matthew 9:21—'IF I MAY BUT TOUCH HIS GARMENT.'

God wants to touch you in the area of your need so when you go out to minister you would be a fit vessel. We overcome by the blood of the Lamb and the word of our testimony. We partake first so we will be a living witness.

MARK 6:56—'THAT THEY MIGHT TOUCH IF IT WERE BUT THE BORDER OF HIS GARMENT; AND AS MANY AS TOUCHED HIM WERE MADE WHOLE.' (KJV)

So many people are saying if God could just touch me in my area of affliction. As you dance in obedience to the Holy Spirit, He will direct you how to make your garments, and as you walk in obedience to Him, you will find that when you dance God will use your garments to touch people and heal them. This has happened so many times while I dance. I would spin down the aisles of the church and my garment would touch people and God would heal them.

HANDS THAT MISTREATED JESUS

Mark 1 4 : 4 1—'… INTO THE HANDS OF SINNERS.'

Remember as dancers God is expecting us to walk worthy of the call for He will keep us from being delivered into the hands of sinners. He said that the righteous can run into Him and be safe.

THE PURPOSE OF THE DANCE

John 18:22—'STRUCK JESUS WITH THE PALM OF HIS HAND …'

When they strike out at you, remember Jesus was also struck at, but it is your response which will show that you are different.

GUILTY HANDS

Proverbs 6:17—'A PROUD LOOK, A LYING TONGUE, HANDS THAT SHED INNOCENT BLOOD.'

Make sure as dancers you do not find yourself caught in idle conversations and talking about other dancers or dance ministries in a negative way. If we are not careful, we can cause death to come into the life of someone by using our tongue.

Proverbs 6:19—'A FALSE WITNESS WHO SPEAKS LIES, AND ONE WHO SOWS DISCORD AMONG BRETHREN.'

Every time we plant a seed, good or bad, we will reap that which we plant, so we must be very careful how we speak when people ask questions about our fellow brother or sister. You must always try to keep unity among the dancers. When someone tries to sow discord, put a stop to it immediately.

Ecclesiastes 10:18—'THROUGH IDLENESS OF THE HANDS …'

Dancers must always find themselves working to the best of their ability to accomplish the vision and goals of the ministry. When we become slack in the things of God we get into idle talk and cause confusion in the dance group.

COMMANDMENTS CONCERNING THE HANDS

IRREVERENT HANDS

Exodus 19:12—'WHOSOEVER TOUCHETH THE MOUNT SHALL BE PUT TO DEATH.'

Most times we take it for granted when God instructs us or give us a command and may disobey Him. God is a holy God and we must be careful how we come before Him and must careful to obey Him. We disrespect Him instead of giving Him reverence, which is due to His name.

Exodus 19:13—'THERE SHALL NOT A HAND TOUCH IT.'

God gave the instruction that no hands should touch the mount. When we don't understand some things that we are instructed to do by our leader, don't ask questions like "Why?" Just be obedient and God will honor your obedience and reward you.

2 Samuel 6 : 6—'UZZAH PUT FORTH HIS HAND.'

There is a penalty for disobeying God. Death is the payment for putting forth our hands to the work of the flesh. Walking in the Spirit will allow us to escape the death penalty.

HANDS OF ANGELS

Psalm 91:12—'IN THEIR HANDS …'

Remember that God has given you angels to assist you in your area of ministry. Wherever you go to minister in dance, do not be afraid, He has you covered. Your hands should be like that of angels, protecting one another as you minister together.

Revelation 10:8—'IN HIS HANDS …'

As the Word is given to us from the hands of our teacher, we must eat it and continue to meditate on it day and night. Then as we minister, the prophetic will flow from us as we dance and the Lord will declare His word through us.

CEREMONIAL CLEANSING OF THE HANDS DOES NOT ASSUAGE GUILT

Matthew 15:2—'FOR THEY WASH NOT THEIR HANDS WHEN THEY EAT BREAD.'

The Lord is more concerned about you eating the bread of life, for it's the Word that will cleanse you and make you whole.

Matthew 27:24—'… WASH HIS HANDS …'

Be sure every one in the dance group ministers with clean hands and a pure heart. Don't let anyone's blood be upon your hands. We are ministers of the Word.

REVIEW OF CHAPTER 5

1. In times of warfare and intercession, a dancer must be _____ using the _____ to pull down the strongholds of the enemy.

2. God will teach our _____ to fight and our _____ to war.

3. Isaiah 52:11—"Depart, depart! Go out from there! _____ no unclean thing, come out from it and be pure, you who carry the vessels of the Lord."

4. The _____ which brings healing can flow through the _____.

5. Psalm 47:1—"_____ your hands all ye people."

6. Dancers are to minister with _____ hands and _____ hearts.

CHAPTER 6

THE DANCER'S FEET

Luke 10:19

"Behold, I give unto you power to tread on serpents and scorpions, and over all the power of the enemy: and nothing shall by any means hurt you."

God has given us the power and authority to use the feet. That is why dance is so effective. The feet uphold the whole body as we go into warfare or worship in the dance. The enemy fears the feet that war.

THE FEET THAT TREAD

I   THE AUTHORITY OF THE FEET

1.   Joshua 10:24

"Come here, put your foot on the neck of these kings."

To humiliate an enemy utterly, one sometimes puts his foot upon the captive's neck, as Joshua's captains did. As we dance, we must remember the devil is under our feet. We must always take authority over him by putting our feet on his neck as we dance.

2.   Malachi 4:3

"And ye shall tread down the wicked; for they shall be ashes under the soles of your feet in the day that I shall do this, saith the Lord of Hosts."

3.   Luke 10:19

"Behold I give you power to tread on serpents and scorpions and over all the power of the enemy and nothing shall by any means harm you."

4.   Romans 16:20

"The God of peace will soon crush Satan under your feet."

Remember, God says the battle is not yours, it's His. We as dancers are to be obedient and led by the Holy Spirit. The Lord will fight for us. Just use your body as an instrument or weapon of war.

5.   Psalm 108:13

"With God we will gain victory and He will trample down our enemies."

If God is for us, who can be against us? No one.

II. SERVANT'S FEET

1. Isaiah 52:7

Isaiah 52:7—"How beautiful upon the mountain are the feet of him who brings good news, who proclaims peace, who brings glad tidings of good things, who proclaims salvation, who says to Zion, Your God reigns!"

2. Nahum 1:15

"Behold upon the mountains the feet of him that bringeth good tidings."

The dancer carries the good news as a servant of God where ever the Lord takes you, always be prepared he might take you from one neighborhood to the next neighborhood or from one city to the other or from one nation to the other nation. Be prepared at all times.

3. Luke 17:9

"To give light to them that sit in darkness and in the shadow of death, to guide our feet into the way of peace."

When we are guided by the Lord, we will be at peace in whatever we do or whatever move we make concerning our ministry.

III. PROTECTION OF THE FEET

1. Psalm 119:101

"I have kept my feet from every evil path so that I may obey your word."

2. Psalm 1:1

God's word is our protection. Walk not in the way of the wicked. Then we are protected.

3.   Psalm 116:8

"For thou has delivered my soul from death, mine eyes from tears, and my feet from falling."

4.   Psalm 119:105

"Thy word is a lamp unto my feet and a light for my path."

5.   Proverbs 3:23 (NIV)

"Then you will go on your way in safety and your foot will not stumble."

REVIEW OF CHAPTER 6

1. The enemy fears the _____ that war.

2. Luke 10:19—"Behold I give you power to _____ upon serpents and scorpions and over all the power of the enemy and nothing shall by any means harm you."

3. To humiliate an enemy, one sometimes puts his _____ upon the captive's neck.

4. As we dance we must remember the devil is under our _____.

5. Isaiah 52:7—"How beautiful upon the mountain are the _____ of him who brings good news, who proclaims _____, who brings glad tidings of _____ things, who proclaims _____, who says to Zion, Your God _____!"

6. The God of peace will soon crush satan under your _____.

CHAPTER 7

HOW TO BECOME AN EFFECTIVE DANCE MINISTER

BECOME BORN AGAIN (A NEW CREATURE)

1. Confess with your mouth that Jesus is Lord. (Romans 10:9)

2. In Christ, neither circumcision availeth anything nor uncircumcision, but a new creature. (Gal. 6: 15)

3. Therefore if any man be in Christ he is a new creature; old things are passed away behold all things have become new.

STUDY THE WORD

1. Study to show thyself approved unto God, a workman who needeth not to be ashamed, rightly dividing the word of truth. (II Timothy 2:15)

HUMBLE YOURSELF

1. God gives grace to the humble. (1 Peter 5:5)

2. Humble yourselves under the mighty hand of God and He will exalt you in due time. (1 Peter 5:6)

3. I dwell in the high and holy place with him also that is of a contrite and humble spirit to revive the heart of the contrite ones. (Isa. 57: 15)

4. Better it is to be of a humble spirit with the lowly, than to divide the spoil with the proud. (Prov. 16: 19)

SUBMIT TO AUTHORITY

Obey your leaders who have rule over you and submit yourselves, for they watch for your souls as they give account, that they may do it with joy and not with grief, for that is unprofitable for you. (Heb. 13: 17)

RESPECT YOUR LEADERS AND HONOR THEM

Render therefore to all their dues, tribute to whom tribute, custom to whom custom, fear to whom fear and honor to whom honor is due (Romans 13:7)

STAY COMMITTED TO THE CALL AND VISION

Where there is no vision the people perish. (Prov. 29: 18)

LEARN TO BE UNIFIED

Behold how good and pleasant it is for brethren to dwell together in unity. It is like the precious ointment upon the head, that ran down upon the beard even Aaron's beard that went down to the skirts of his garments.

REVIEW OF CHAPTER 7

1. To be an effective dance minister you must first be

   _____ .

2. We must study the _____ of God.

3. God gives grace to the _____ .

4. _____ your leaders who have rule over you

   and _____ yourselves.

5. Stay committed to the _____ and

   _____ .

6. Learn to be _____ .

7. Behold how _____ and _____

   it is for brethren to dwell together in _____ .

GENERAL REVIEW

1. Dance is of _____.

2. We are commanded to praise the Lord in the _____ _____.

3. Dance must bring glory to _____.

4. When we dance, we dance before the _____ of kings.

5. God is seeking for _____ worshippers in the dance.

6. The Dance of War involves movement of the _____ and _____ with power and strength.

THE PURPOSE OF THE DANCE

7. God's desire is for us to use our gift of dance to draw people to

   _____.

8. The dance ought to bring _____, deliverance

   and _____ to souls.

978-0-595-48174-3
0-595-48174-4

CPSIA information can be obtained at www.ICGtesting.com
Printed in the USA
270624BV00002B/69/P